# Georg Friedr Handel

## Six Sonatas for Flute or Violin and Piano

T0085279

## CONTENTS

To access audio visit:
**www.halleonard.com/mylibrary**

Enter Code
6418-2626-2503-2345

ISBN 978-1-59615-663-0

Music Minus One

Exclusively Distributed By

HAL•LEONARD®

Visit Hal Leonard Online at
**www.halleonard.com**

Contact Us:
**Hal Leonard**
7777 West Bluemound Road
Milwaukee, WI 53213
Email: info@halleonard.com

In Europe contact:
**Hal Leonard Europe Limited**
Distribution Centre, Newmarket Road
Bury St Edmunds, Suffolk, IP33 3YB
Email: info@halleonardeurope.com

In Australia contact:
**Hal Leonard Australia Pty. Ltd.**
4 Lentara Court
Cheltenham, Victoria, 3192 Australia
Email: info@halleonard.com.au

# SONATA IN A MAJOR
## OP. 1, NO. 3

Georg Friedrich Händel
(1685-1759)

8 taps (1 measure) precede music.

4

4 taps ( 1 measure ) precede music.

**Allegro.**

# Sonata in G Minor

## Op. 1, No. 10

Georg Friedrich Händel
(1685-1759)

8 taps (1 measure) precede music.

**Allegretto.** 4 taps (1 measure) precede music.

# SONATA IN F MAJOR
## OP. 1, NO. 12

Georg Friedrich Händel
(1685-1759)

**Adagio.** 3 taps (1 measure) precede music.

**Allegro.** 4 taps (1 measure) precede music.

# SONATA IN D MAJOR
## OP. 1, NO. 13

Georg Friedrich Händel
(1685-1759)

**Allegro.** ∠ 4 taps (1 measure) precede music.

# SONATA IN A MAJOR
## OP. 1, NO. 14

Georg Friedrich Händel
(1685-1759)

# Sonata in E Major

## Op. 1, No. 15

Georg Friedrich Händel
(1685-1759)

**Allegro.** 4 taps (2 measures) precede music.

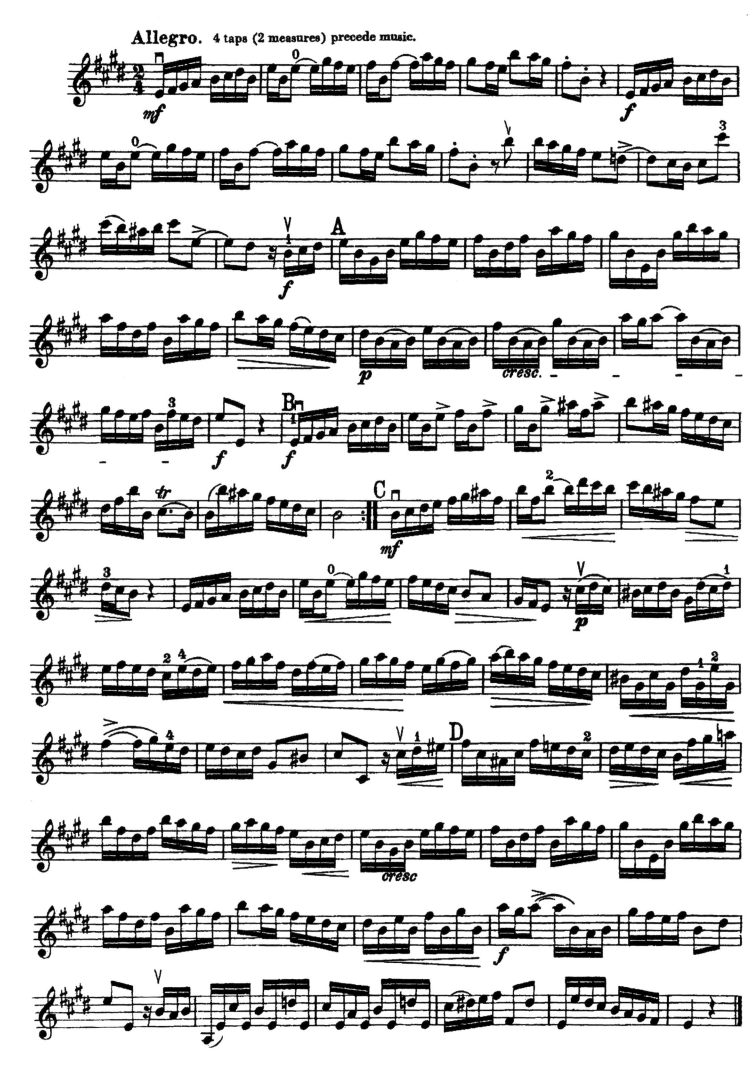

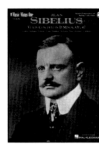

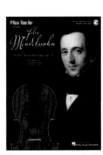

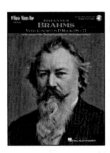